Festivals

My Easter

Jennifer Blizin Gillis

Raintree

Chicago, Illinois

© 2006 Raintree
a division of Reed Elsevier Inc.
Chicago, Illinois

Customer Service 888-363-4266
Visit our website at www.raintreelibrary.com

Designed by Joanna Hinton-Malivoire and Tokay
Printed and bound in China by South China Printing Company

10 09 08 07 06
10 9 8 7 6 5 4 3 2 1

Library of Congress Cataloging-in-Publication Data
Gillis, Jennifer Blizin, 1950-
   My Easter / Jennifer Blizin Gillis.-- 1st ed.
      p. cm. -- (Festivals)
   Includes bibliographical references and index.
   ISBN 1-4109-0780-5 (hc) -- ISBN 1-4109-0785-6 (pb)
   1. Easter--Juvenile literature. I. Title. II. Series: Festivals
(Raintree Publishers)
   GT4935.G55 2005
   394.2667--dc22
                                     2004022901

Acknowledgments
The author and publisher are grateful to the following for permission to reproduce copyright material:
AP Wide World Photo pp.**21** (Hiroko Masuike); Corbis pp.**4** (Philip James Corwin), **6**, **10** (Ariel Skelley),
11 (James Marshall), **16** (Ariel Skelley); Foodpix pp.**12** (Thomas Firak), **23** (Triolo Productions/Burke);
Getty Images pp.**5** (Photodisc Blue), **7** (FoodPix/Amy Neunsinger), **13** (Photodisc Green), **17** (The
Image Bank/Ross Whitaker), **18** (Photodisc Green/C Squared Studios), **19** (Botanica/Eleonara Ghioldi);
Index Stock pp.**9** (David H. Smith); Photo Edit, Inc. pp.**8** (James Shaffer), **20** (Robert Brenner);
PictureQuest/Stockbyte pp.**14–15**, **22**.

Cover photograph reproduced with permission of Getty Images/Photodisc Green.

Some words are shown in bold, **like this**. You can find out
what they mean by looking in the glossary on page 24.

Contents

The calendar shows when it will be Easter.

Today Is
/12
Easter Sunday
Sat./Sun.
April

Easter is always on a Sunday.

Getting Ready

We clean the house.

We make special
Easter treats.

7

New Things for Easter

Mom and dad buy us new clothes.

We buy big baskets.

Easter Flowers

People buy Easter flowers to **decorate** their houses.

We will buy this Easter **lily** for grandma.

These Easter lilies are growing in a **greenhouse**.

Then, we **dye** the eggs
with **food color**.

Easter Morning

We wake up on Easter morning.

Look at our
Easter baskets!

15

Easter eggs are good for Easter breakfast.

17

Easter Candy

We get a lot of candy for Easter.

Mom lets us eat one piece
of candy after breakfast.

19

Easter Parade

There is an Easter parade in our city.

We **decorate** hats and wear them.

21

Easter Dinner

Grandma and grandpa come for Easter dinner.

We will eat this big, juicy ham.

Glossary

bloom grow into a flower

decorate make more beautiful by adding something

dye give a new color

food color color for food that you can eat

greenhouse glass building used to grow plants

hunt trying to find something

lily Kind of flower. Easter lilies are white and grow in spring

spring one of four seasons in a year. Spring months are March, April, and May.

Index